CENGAGE Learning

Short Stories for Students, Volume 4

Staff

Editorial: Kathleen Wilson, Marie Lazzari, *Editors.* Greg Barnhisel, Thomas Bertonneau, Cynthia Bily, Paul Bodine, Julia Burch, Yoonmee Chang, John Chua, Carol Dell'Amico, Catherine Dominic, Mark Elliot, Terry Girard, Rena Korb, Rebecca Laroche, *Sketchwriters.* Suzanne Dewsbury, James Person, *Contributing Editors.* Aarti Stephens, *Managing Editor*

Research: Victoria B. Cariappa, *Research Manager.* Andrew Malonis, *Research Specialist.*

Permissions: Susan M. Trosky, *Permissions Manager.* Kimberly Smilay, *Permissions Specialist.* Kelly Quin, *Permissions Associate.*

Production: Mary Beth Trimper, *Production Director.* Evi Seoud, *Assistant Production Manager.* Shanna Heilveil, *Production Assistant*

Graphic Services: Randy Bassett, *Image Database Supervisor.* Mikal Ansari, Robert Duncan, *Imaging Specialists.* Pamela A. Reed, *Photography Coordinator.*

Copyright Notice

Copyright 1998
Gale Research
835 Penobscot Building
645 Griswold
Detroit, MI 48226-4094

This book is printed on acid-free paper that meets the minimum requirements of American National Standard for Information Sciences—Permanence Paper for Printed Library Materials, ANSI Z39.48-1984.

ISBN 0-7876-2219-2
ISSN 1092-7735

Printed in the United States of America
10 9 8 7 6 5 4 3 2 1

The Tell-Tale Heart

Edgar Allan Poe

1843

Introduction

One of Edgar Allan Poe's most famous short stories, "The Tell-Tale Heart," was first published in the January, 1843 edition of James Russell Lowell's *The Pioneer* and was reprinted in the August 23, 1845 issue of *The Broadway Journal.* The story is a psychological portrait of a mad narrator who kills a man and afterward hears his victim's relentless heartbeat. While "The Tell-Tale Heart" and his other short stories were not critically acclaimed during his lifetime, Poe earned respect among his peers as a competent writer, insightful literary critic, and gifted poet, particularly after the publication of his famous poem, "The Raven," in 1845.

After Poe's death in 1849, some critics faulted his obsession with dark and depraved themes. Other critics, like George Woodberry in his 1885 study of Poe, considered "The Tell-Tale Heart" merely a "tale of conscience." But this simplistic view has changed over the years as more complex views of Poe and his works have emerged. Poe is now considered a forefather of two literary genres, detective stories and science fiction, and is regarded as an important writer of psychological thrillers and horror.

"The Tell-Tale Heart" is simultaneously a horror story and psychological thriller told from a first-person perspective. It is admired as an excellent example of how a short story can produce an effect on the reader. Poe believed that all good literature must create a unity of effect on the reader and this effect must reveal truth or evoke emotions. "The Tell-Tale Heart" exemplifies Poe's ability to expose the dark side of humankind and is a harbinger of novels and films dealing with psychological realism. Poe's work has influenced genres as diverse as French symbolist poetry and Hollywood horror films, and writers as diverse as Ambrose Bierce and Sir Arthur Conan Doyle.

Author Biography

Edgar Allan Poe was born into a theatrical family on January 19, 1809. His father, David Poe, was a lawyer-turned-actor, and his mother, Elizabeth Arnold, was an English actress. Both his parents died before Poe turned three years old, and he was raised by John Allan, a rich businessman, in Richmond, Virginia. Allan never legally adopted Poe, and their relationship became a stormy one after Poe reached his teenage years.

Unlike the narrator in "The Tell-Tale Heart," who claims that he had no desires for the old man's gold, Poe was dependent on Allan for financial support. While Allan funded Poe's education at a private school in England for five years, he failed to support him when he attended the University of Virginia and the United States Military Academy at West Point. Aware that he would never inherit much from his prosperous foster father, Poe embarked on a literary career at the age of twenty-one.

In 1835, Poe secretly married his thirteen-year-old cousin, Virginia Clemm. For the next two years, he worked as an assistant editor for the *Southern Literary Messenger* while publishing fiction and book reviews. He was ill-suited for editorial work. Like his natural father, Poe was an alcoholic. Dismissed by his employer, Poe moved to New York City and later to Philadelphia. He published several works, including "The Narrative of Arthur Gordon Pym" in 1838, "The Fall of the House of Usher" in 1839, and "The Tell-Tale Heart" in 1843. While his writings were well regarded, his financial position was constantly precarious. Poe took on a series of editorial positions, but his alcoholism and contentious temper continued to plague him. In 1845 Poe published "The Raven," his most famous poem. Celebrated as a gifted poet, he failed to win many friends due to his unpleasant temperament. After his wife's death from tuberculosis in 1847, Poe became involved in a number of romances, including one with Elmira Royster that had been interrupted in his youth. Now Elmira was the widowed Mrs. Shelton. It was during the time they were preparing for their marriage that Poe, for reasons unknown, arrived in Baltimore in late September of 1849. On October 3, he was discovered in a state of semiconsciousness. He died on October 7 without being able to explain what had happened during the last days of his life.

Upon Poe's death in 1849, his one-time friend and literary executor, R. W. Griswold, wrote a libelous obituary in the *New York Tribune* defaming Poe by attributing the psychological conditions of many of his literary characters to Poe's own state of mind. Most critics, however, contend that there is nothing to suggest that Poe psychologically resembled any of his emotionally and mentally unstable fictitious characters. Indeed, he took pride in demonstrating his keen intellect in his "tales of ratiocination."

Plot Summary

"The Tell-Tale Heart" begins with the famous line "True!—nervous—very, very nervous I had been and am; but why *will* you say that I am mad?" The narrator insists that his disease has sharpened, not dulled, his senses. He tells the tale of how an old man who lives in his house has never wronged him. For an unknown reason, the old man's cloudy, pale blue eye has incited madness in the narrator. Whenever the old man looks at him, his blood turns cold. Thus, he is determined to kill him to get rid of this curse.

Again, the narrator argues that he is not mad. He claims the fact that he has proceeded cautiously indicates that he is sane. For a whole week, he has snuck into the man's room every night, but the victim has been sound asleep with his eyes closed each time. The narrator cannot bring himself to kill the man without seeing his "Evil Eye." On the eighth night, however, the man springs up and cries "Who's there?" In the dark room, the narrator waits silently for an hour. The man does not go back to sleep; instead, he gives out a slight groan, realizing that "Death" is approaching. Eventually, the narrator shines his lamp on the old man's eye. The narrator immediately becomes furious at the "damned spot," but he soon hears the beating of a heart so loud that he fears the neighbors will hear it. With a yell, he leaps into the room and kills the old man. Despite the murder, he continues to hear the man's relentless heartbeat.

He dismembers the corpse and hides the body parts beneath the floorboards. There is a knock on the front door; the police have come to investigate a shriek the neighbors have reported. The narrator invites them to search the premises. He blames his scream on a bad dream and explains that the old man is not home. The officers are satisfied but refuse to leave. Soon the sound of the heartbeat resumes, growing more and more distinct. The narrator grows pale and raises his voice to muffle the sound. At last, unable to stand it any longer, the narrator screams: "I admit the deed!—tear up the planks!—here, here!—it is the beating of his hideous heart!"

Characters

Narrator

The narrator of "The Tell-Tale Heart" recounts his murder of an old man. Since he tells the story in first-person, the reader cannot determine how much of what he says is true; thus, he is an unreliable narrator. Though he repeatedly states that he is sane, the reader suspects otherwise from his bizarre reasoning, behavior, and speech. He speaks with trepidation from the famous first line of the story: "True—nervous—very, very dreadfully nervous I had been and am; but why *will* you say that I am mad?" The reader soon realizes through Poe's jolting description of the narrator's state of mind that the protagonist has in fact descended into madness. The narrator claims that he loves the old man and has no motive for the murder other than growing dislike of a cloudy film over one of the old man's eyes. Poe effectively conveys panic in the narrator's voice, and the reader senses uneasiness and growing tension in the narrative. Through the first-person narrative of a madman, Poe effectively creates a gothic tale full of horror and psychological torment, a style he termed "arabesque."

Old man

The old man is known to readers only through the narration of the insane protagonist. According to the narrator, the old man had never done anything to warrant his murder. However, the old man's cloudy, pale blue eye bothers the narrator tremendously. The narrator believes that only by killing the old man can he get rid of the eye's overpowering malignant force. The old man is apparently quite rich, for he possesses "treasures" and "gold" and he locks the window shutters in his room for fear of robbers. However, the narrator states that he has no desire for his gold. In fact, he claims that he loves the old man. Through the narrator, the reader understands the horror that the old man experiences as he realizes that his companion is about to kill him. The narrator claims that he too knows this horror very well. Some critics argue that the old man must have known about the narrator's violent tendencies, for he cries out in horror well before the narrator kills him. Other critics suggest that the old man may have been the narrator's guardian or even father. Still other critics believe that the old man is a doppelganger for the narrator, that is, he is his double, and the narrator's loathing for the man represents his own self-loathing.

Guilt and Innocence

The guilt of the narrator is a major theme in "The Tell-Tale Heart." The story is about a mad person who, after killing a companion for no apparent reason, hears an interminable heartbeat and releases his overwhelming sense of guilt by shouting his confession to the police. Indeed, some early critics saw the story as a straightforward parable about self-betrayal by the criminal's conscience.

Media Adaptations

- *Listen & Read Edgar Allan Poe's "The Tell-Tale Heart" and Other Stories* is an audio-cassette recording packaged with a book. Produced by Dover Press, 1996.

- "The Tell-Tale Heart" was adapted into a black-and-white film starring Sam Jaffe in 1980. It is available on video from Facets Multimedia, Chicago.

- In 1934, "The Tell-Tale Heart" was made into a movie entitled *Bucket of Blood* starring John Kelt as The Old Man and Norman Dryden as the protagonist.

- In 1956 producer/director Lee W. Wilder loosely adapted two of Poe's stories, "The Gold Bug" and "The Tell-Tale Heart," in his movie *Manfish.*

- In 1962, "The Tell-Tale Heart" was made into a British movie by director Ernest Morris. Known as *The Tell-Tale Heart,* it also carries the alternate title *The Hidden Room of 1,000 Horrors.* It is available on video from Nostalgia Family Video.

- In 1969, "The Tell-Tale Heart" was made into an animated film narrated by actor James Mason. A Columbia Pictures release, it is also available on video.

- Another audio recording is available from Downsview of Ontario,

Canada. *Tales of Mystery and Horror* features the voice of actor Christopher Lee. Produced in 1981.

The narrator never pretends to be innocent, fully admitting that he has killed the old man because of the victim's pale blue, film-covered eye which the narrator believes to be a malignant force. The narrator suggests that there are uncontrollable forces which can drive people to commit violent acts. In the end, however, Poe's skillful writing allows the reader to sympathize with the narrator's miserable state despite fully recognizing that he is guilty by reason of insanity.

Sanity and Insanity

Closely related to the theme of guilt and innocence is the issue of sanity. From the first line of the story—"True!—nervous—very, very dreadfully nervous I had been and am, but why *will* you say that I am mad?"—the reader recognizes that something strange has occurred. His obsession with conveying to his audience that he is sane only amplifies his lack of sanity. The first tangible sign that the narrator is indeed mad appears in the second paragraph, when he compares the old man's eye to a vulture's eye. He explains his decision to "take the life of the old man" in order to free himself from the curse of the eye. The narrator's argument that he is sane, calculating, and methodical is unconvincing, however, and his erratic and confused language suggests that he is disordered. Thus, what the narrator considers to be evidence of a sane person—the meticulous and thoughtful plans required to carry out a ghastly and unpleasant deed—are interpreted instead by the reader to be manifestations of insanity.

Time

A secondary theme in "The Tell-Tale Heart" is the role of time as a pervasive force throughout the story. Some critics note that the narrator is obsessed with time. While the entire narrative is told as one long flashback, the narrator is painfully aware of the agonizing effect on him of time. Although the action in this narrative occurs mainly during one long night, the numerous references the narrator makes to time show that the horror he experiences has been building over time. From the beginning, he explains that his obsession with ridding the curse of the eye has "haunted [him] day and night." For seven long nights the narrator waits for the right moment to murder his victim. When on the eighth night the old man realizes that someone is in his room, the narrator remains still for an entire hour. The old man's terror is also felt by the narrator, who had endured "night after night hearkening to the death watches in the wall." (Death watches are a type of small beetle that live in wood and make a ticking sound.)

For the narrator, death and time are closely linked. He explains that "the old man's hour had come," all the while painfully aware of the hours it takes to kill a victim and clean up the scene of the crime. What drives the narrator over the edge is hearing the overwhelming sound of a heartbeat, which he compares to "a low, dull, quick sound, such as a watch makes when enveloped in cotton." Yet after killing the old man, the narrator says that for "many minutes, the heart beat on." He repeats his comparison of the heartbeat to a ticking watch as the unrelenting sound drives him to confess to the police. The narrator's hour has also arrived.

Style

Point of View

A notable aspect of "The Tell-Tale Heart" is that the story is told from the first-person point of view. The story is a monologue of a nervous narrator telling the reader how he murdered someone. He is eventually driven to confess to the police. The entire straightforward narrative is told from his point of view in a nervous tone. Through Poe's masterful and inventive writing, the narrator's twisted logic increasingly reveals that he is insane. By using a first-person narrative, Poe heightens the tension and fear running through the mind of the narrator. There is a clear connection between the language used by the narrator and his psychological state. The narrator switches between calm, logical statements and quick, irrational outbursts. His use of frequent exclamations reveals his extreme nervousness. The first-person point of view draws the reader into the mind of the insane narrator, enabling one to ironically sympathize with his wretched state of mind. Some critics suggest that the entire narrative represents a kind of confession, as at a trial or police station. Others consider the first-person point of view as a logical way to present a parable of self-betrayal by the criminal's conscience—a remarkable record of the voice of a guilty mind.

Topics for Further Study

- Research the illnesses of schizophrenia and paranoia. Do you think the protagonist suffers from either of these conditions? Why or why not?

- Research how Manifest Destiny was a pervasive ideology in mid-nineteenth century America. How does "The Tell-Tale Heart" challenge the rationalism and optimism of a young nation?

- "The Tell-Tale Heart" was written more than 150 years ago. Why do you think it is still widely read today? What are some elements of the story which make it timeless? What makes a classic literary or artistic work?

Denouement

The denouement, or the resolution, of the narrative occurs in "The Tell-Tale Heart" when the narrator, prompted by the incessant sound of a beating heart, can no longer contain his ever-increasing sense of guilt. Poe is regarded by literary critics as having helped define the architecture of the modern short story, in which its brevity requires an economical use of sentences and paragraphs and the climactic ending often occurs in the last paragraph. The abrupt ending in this story is calculated to concentrate an effect on the reader. In "The Tell-Tale Heart" the crisis of conscience is resolved when the murderer shrieks the last lines of the story: "I admit the deed!—tear up the planks!—here, here!—it is the beating of his hideous heart!" This abrupt outburst is a shock to the reader, a sudden bursting of the tension that has filled the story, and it provides the dramatic, emotional conclusion to the story.

Aestheticism and Arabesque

Poe was a writer concerned more with style and mood than his American contemporaries were, like James Fenimore Cooper, whose fiction was often morally didactic. Poe believed that a story should create a mood in a reader, or evoke emotions in order to be successful, and that it should not try to teach the reader a lesson. He called his style "arabesque," and it was notable for its ornate, intricate prose that sought to create a feeling of unsettlement in the reader. This arabesque prose became a primary component of the "art for art's sake" movement, known as Aestheticism, that began in France in the nineteenth century. Poe's works were highly esteemed by French writers, like the poet Charles Baudelaire, and their emulation of his style eventually influenced the Symbolists and helped bring an end to the Victorian age in literature. In "The Tell-Tale Heart," an example of arabesque prose is when the narrator describes sneaking into the old man's room in the middle of the night: "I heard a slight groan, and I knew it was the groan of mortal terror. It was not a groan of pain or of grief—oh no!—it was the low stifled sound that arises from the bottom of the soul when overcharged with awe." Instead of simply stating that he had heard a groan, the narrator describes the sound in detail, creating in the reader a sense of suspense and foreboding.

Doppelganger

In literature, a doppelganger is a character that functions as the main character's double in order to highlight the main character's personality or act as a foil to it. Some critics have maintained that in "The Tell-Tale Heart," the old man functions as a doppelganger to the narrator. Thus, the narrator is truly mad, and he kills the old man because he cannot stand himself, perhaps fearing becoming old or disfigured like him. The narrator recounts evidence to support this idea: he does not hate the man, in fact, he professes to love him; on the eighth night when the narrator sneaks into his room, the old man awakens, sits bolt upright in bed and listens in silence for an hour in the darkness, as does the narrator. Most notably, when the old man begins to moan, the narrator admits that the same sound had "welled up from my own bosom" many nights. When he hears the man's heart quicken with terror, he admits that he is nervous, too. Other critics have maintained that the old man does not exist. After all, the narrator tells police that it was he who screamed, and it is not stated that the police actually found a body. According to this viewpoint, the old man's cloudy eye is nothing more than a twisted fixation of the narrator's own mind, and the relentless heartbeat is not the old man's, but the narrator's.

Literature in the 19th Century

Poe wrote at a time when the United States was experiencing rapid economical and geographical expansion. During the mid-nineteenth century, the most popular authors in the growing United States were those who wrote adventure fiction. American nautical explorations (particularly of the Pacific region) and westward expansion captured the imagination of the public. Such Poe stories as "A Descent into the Maelstrom" and "The Gold Bug" reflect the public's fascination with adventures at home and abroad. Poe's America was a vibrant and self-assured young nation with a firm belief in its manifest destiny. James Fenimore Cooper's *The Last of the Mohicans,* which outlined the moral struggles of an expanding country, was a moral tale that pitted the white man against Native Americans. Herman Melville was a favorite with readers, with his novels of sea-faring life, which often paled in comparison to the adventures of his own youth. Long, action-oriented novels such as these were a primary form of entertainment for many people. Washington Irving, who lived and wrote in the emerging metropolis of New York City, began to catalogue some of the arising American folklore in his tales and stories, although he frequently traveled in Europe to gather material for his writing and followed a tradition British format in his prose.

Novels in this era typically imitated British literature until new themes arose from authors who were distinctly American. Poe was one of the first to create a distinctly American literature. In his short stories, particularly, he sought to fashion tales of terror based on mood and language. He also helped popularize the short story form, and soon many magazines were being published that provided their audiences with new stories every month. The magazines became an important part of popular life, and Poe published many stories in them, though few brought him solid popularity. Through his short stories, especially "Murders in the Rue Morgue" Poe became one of the first practitioners of the detective story, in which a mystery is presented that must be solved by an observant inspector, whose viewpoint is also that of the reader's.

Psychological Elements of Poe's Fiction

Historians note that Poe's writings emphasizing the dark side of humanity and nature challenged the optimistic and confident spirit of the American people during the nineteenth century. Scientific progress and rational thought were revolutionizing industry and agriculture. For example, such nineteenth-century creations as steamships expanded commerce, while steel plows and the McCormick reapers increased agricultural production manyfold. Poe, like other writers of his time, was influenced by the exaggerated emotions and sombre moods of Romanticism, but he differs from his contemporaries in a number of ways. While Poe does not reject rational science (his "tales of ratiocination" herald the triumph of the superior rational mind), he undermines the faith in rationality in some of his stories. "The Tell-Tale Heart" tells of a man who ironically (and perhaps also paradoxically) strongly believes in the need for making methodical and calculated decisions but is eventually overcome by inexplicable psychological forces that stem from his irrational, unstable nature. Thus, while Poe's works display a strong interest in rational science, his writings also explore the psychologically unfathomable aspects of the human condition and the inexplicable elements of the universe.

Compare & Contrast

- **1840s:** Mental illness is thought to be related to immoral behavior or the physical degeneration of the central nervous system. Insanity is thought to be the result of such diseases as syphilis.

  1990s: After years of institutionalizing mentally ill patients and subjecting them to electroshock therapy, modern treatment of mental illness such as depression, bi-polar disorder, and schizophrenia include counseling and drug therapy.

- **1840s:** "The Tell-Tale Heart" is published in 1843. The story is a psychological thriller that invites the reader into the world of the narrator's insanity. Other examples of Poe's eerie, macabre style include "The Pit and the Pendulum," written in 1842, which explores the dark side of human nature and features both cruelty and torture.

  1990s: People continue to be fascinated by the dark side of humanity. The popular film *Silence of the Lambs* examines the psychological motivations of a serial killer. Best-selling author Stephen King, along with other horror writers, explores the supernatural, the paranormal, and the way in which seemingly ordinary events can suddenly turn into terrifying encounters with psychotic killers.

Poe differs from writers of his time in one other significant way. "The Tell-Tale Heart" is an example of how his writing produces a psychological effect. While his contemporaries generally regarded a story's moral or ideological position as paramount, Poe believed that the aim of literature is to reveal truth or elicit an emotional or psychological reaction. Poe also rejected the emphasis by his contemporaries on the utilitarian value of literature. He considered their ideological view a "heresy of the Didactic." Instead, Poe proposed an ideology of "art for art's sake," with style and aesthetics playing prominent roles. Literary critics and historians now consider Poe as one of the architects of the modern short story. Indeed, Poe proposes that a short literary work can use its brevity to concentrate a unified effect on the reader. Poe's precise and controlled language works to produce a particular effect on the reader. Writers of poetry and short fiction since Poe have generally acknowledged his maxim as fundamental. Poe's works have influenced many writers, including Baudelaire and Ambrose Bierce, and such literary movements as the French Symbolists and Surrealists.

Critical Overview

During his lifetime, Poe's greatest recognition came from France. Charles Baudelaire translated and commented on Poe's stories in the 1850s. Baudelaire was a famous French writer in his own right, and his translations are considered by a few critics to be superior to Poe's original prose. These translations popularized Poe in France, bringing him wide fame and influence. In the later half of the nineteenth century, the psychological aspects of Poe's writings influenced French Symbolist poets. In the United States, however, Poe was often criticized for his stories. Many writers thought that they were overly emotional and contained no good lessons or stories. Poe never made much money from his fiction, although he had limited success as a poet.

In the generations since his death, however, critics have come to fully appreciate Poe's works. His poetry continues to be popular, and he is now regarded as an early master of the short story, particularly for his contributions to the detective and horror genres, of which "The Tell-Tale Heart" is a prime example. One of the reasons why he is so highly regarded is because his stories are open to so many different interpretations, a factor that was not appreciated in his day. Contemporary critics acknowledge that "The Tell-Tale Heart" can be read as a classic example of American Gothicism, a morality tale, a supernatural story, a criticism of rationalism, and a multi-level psychological narrative. The full dimension and nuances of this tale are explored in James Gargano's "The Theme of Time in 'The Tell-Tale Heart'." Gargano proposes that "The Tell-Tale Heart" is more complicated than it might first appear because Poe laces the story with "internally consistent symbols that are charged with meaning" and because the narrator is unreliable, causing the reader to question the veracity of his story. E. Arthur Robinson explores the idea of the doppelganger in his essay "Poe's 'The Tell-Tale Heart'," claiming that the narrator and the old man identify closely with each other and arguing that beneath the flow of the narration, "the story illustrates the elaboration of design which Poe customarily sought."

While two of Poe's stories, "MS. Found in a Bottle" and "The Gold Bug" were critically well received, each winning a prize during Poe's lifetime, "The Tell-Tale Heart" obtained no special recognition. Poe's contemporaries accorded him respect as a talented poet, literary critic and fiction writer. Some of his works received a measure of popular success, particularly "The Raven," his most well known poem, which was first published in 1845. However, temperamentally unpleasant and a chronic alcoholic, Poe did not handle his success well, alienating some of his potential supporters.

Some early critics saw the psychologically unbalanced state of his fictional characters as an extension of Poe's own mental state. His literary executor, R. W. Griswold, wrote a libelous obituary in the *New York Tribune* vilifying him as mentally depraved. Even as late as 1924, critic Alfred C. Ward, writing about "The Tell-Tale Heart" in *Aspects of the Modern Short Story: English and American* argued that Poe "had ever before him the aberrations of his own troubled mind—doubtfully poised at all times, perhaps, and almost certainly subject to more or less frequent periods of disorder: consequently, it was probably more nearly normal, for him, to picture the abnormal than to depict the average." Other early critics considered stories such as "The Tell-Tale Heart" basically self-explanatory. One nineteenth century critic, George Woodberry, simply called it a "tale of conscience" in his 1885 study, *Edgar Allan Poe.*

Although "The Tell-Tale Heart" did not receive much recognition during the author's lifetime, its status has gained steadily since his death. Now among one of his most widely read works, the tale adds to Poe's reputation as an innovator of literary form, technique, and vision. Almost every important American writer since Poe shows signs of his influence, particularly those writing gothic fiction and grotesque satires and humor.

What Do I Read Next?

- "Young Goodman Brown" (1835) by Nathaniel Hawthorne concerns a newly married man who must leave home on a short journey. While walking through the woods, he encounters the townspeople engaged in a satanic ritual. This vision destroys Goodman Brown, though it is never clear whether he actually saw the things he claimed, or just imagined them.

- "The Monkey's Paw" (1902) by W. W. Jacobs is the story about a Sergeant-Major who brings a monkey's paw back from his travels in India. He presents it to the White family, who joke about its supposed power to grant the owner three wishes. The Whites's careless wishes lead to tragedy and horror.

- "The Secret Sharer" (1909) by Joseph Conrad is the story of a young sea captain who knowingly harbors a stowaway on his ship. The man, who has been accused of murder, serves as a doppelganger for the young captain, and gives him the courage to stand up to his crew, even though the stowaway's life and character remain shrouded in mystery.

- Poe's short story "The Fall of the House of Usher" (1839) also explores the impulses of a deranged protagonist who entombs his sister only to find that she returns to destroy him.

- Poe's "William Wilson" also deals with the lifelong confrontation of a protagonist with a mysterious *doppelganger,* or double.

- *The Turn of the Screw* (1898), a novella by Henry James, tells the story of ghostly apparitions seen by an English governess in Victorian mansion. Some critics interpret the hallucinations as the manifestations of a repressed mind.

Sources

Gargano, James W. "The Theme of Time in 'The Tell-Tale Heart'." *Studies in Short Fiction,* Vol. V, no. 1 (Fall 1967): 378-82.

> "the protagonist's painful insistence
> in 'proving' himself sane only serves
> to intensify the idea of his madness."

Gargano, James W. "The Question of Poe's Narrators." *College English,* Vol. 25, no. 3 (December 1963): 177-81.

Robinson, E. Arthur. "Poe's 'The Tell-Tale Heart'." *Nineteenth-Century Fiction,* Vol. 19, no. 4 (March 1965): 369-78.

Ward, Alfred C. "Edgar Allan Poe: 'Tales of Mystery and Imagination'." *Aspects of the Modern Short Story: English and American,* University of London Press, 1924, pp. 32-44.

Further Reading

Lewis, R. W. B. *Edgar Allan Poe,* Chelsea House, 1997.

A critical study of Poe's works.

Quinn, Arthur Hobsons, and Shawn J. Rosenheim. *Edgar Allan Poe: A Critical Biography,* Johns Hopkins University Press, 1997.

Outlines Poe's life with special emphasis on his works.

Rosenheim, Shawn, and Stephen Rachman. *The American Face of Edgar Allan Poe,* Johns Hopkins University Press, 1995.

Essays on Poe that compare his work to that of Jorge Borges and contemporaries Harriet Beecher Stowe and William Wordsworth. Other essays discuss themes such as psychoanalysis, literary nationalism, and authorial identity as it relates to his work.

Lightning Source UK Ltd.
Milton Keynes UK
UKHW02f1826091018
330276UK00011B/661/P